THE PSYCHOLOGY OF BECOMING A MILLIONAIRE

The Science of Breaking Free
From Paycheck-to-Paycheck
Cycle And Joining The Ranks Of
The Rich Elite

By

CASEY NORMAN

TABLE OF CONTENT

CONCLUSION

PREFACE.

This book is a practical guide, not a theoretical dissertation; it is pragmatic rather than intellectual. It is meant for those men and women whose first need is money; who want to get wealthy first and then become philosophical. It is intended for individuals who have not yet had the time, resources, or chance to delve deeply into the study of metaphysics but who are results-driven and prepared to use scientific findings as a springboard for action without delving into all the steps that led to those findings.

The reader is expected to accept the basic assertions at face value, just as he would accept claims about a law of electrical action if they were made by an Edison or a Marconi. He is also expected to act fearlessly and without hesitation in order to demonstrate the veracity of the assertions. Anyone who follows through on this will undoubtedly become wealthy since the science being used is precise and failure is unimaginable. However, I shall reference certain sources here for the advantage of individuals who would want to study philosophical ideas and thus provide a rational foundation for religion.

The Hindu monistic view of the cosmos, which holds that "One is All and All is One" and that "one Substance manifests itself as the seeming many elements of the material world," has been slowly infiltrating Western philosophy over the last 200 years. All Oriental philosophies, as well as those of Descartes, Spinoza, Leibnitz, Schopenhauer, Hegel, and Emerson, are built upon it.

The reader who wishes to delve to the philosophical roots is recommended to study Hegel and Emerson; and he would do well to read "The Eternal News," a very fine booklet issued by J. J. Brown, 300 Cathcart Road, Govanhill, Glasgow, Scotland. A collection of the author's pieces titled "What is Truth?" that appeared in Nautilus (Holyoke, Mass.) in the spring and summer of 1909 would also be of use to him.

In order for everyone to comprehend this book, I have sacrificed all other factors in favor of language that is clear and simple. The strategy outlined here was derived from philosophical conclusions; it has undergone extensive testing and passed the ultimate test of real-world experimentation; it is effective. study the works of the aforementioned writers to learn how the conclusions were reached. If you want to put their principles into practice, study this book and follow its instructions to the letter.

CHAPTER 1:

The Prerogative to be rich

Whatever the case for poverty, the reality is that without wealth, it is impossible to have a really fulfilled or prosperous life. Without a lot of money, no man can develop his skill or reach his full potential in either area. This is because developing talent and unfolding the soul need a variety of resources, which are only available to those who can afford them.

Man advances in body, mind, and soul via the use of objects, and because society is structured in such a way that a person needs money to become the owner of objects, the science of wealth creation must be the cornerstone of all human progress. Development is the aim of all life, and every living thing has an unalienable right to all the development it can achieve. A man's right to life is, in essence, his right to own all that may be required for his complete mental, spiritual, and physical development; in other words, his right to wealth.

I will not use the term "rich" in a metaphorical sense in this book; being really wealthy does not imply being comfortable or content with a small amount. If a guy can use and enjoy more, he should not be content with a little. Nature exists to promote and develop life, and it is immoral for a man to be satisfied with less than everything that may enhance the strength, grace, beauty, and richness of life.

A guy is affluent if he has all he needs to live the fullest life he can; no one without a large bank account can possess everything they want. Because of how far life has gone and how complicated it has gotten, even the average person needs a significant amount of cash to live a life that even somewhat resembles completion. Human nature is such that the drive to achieve intrinsic capabilities is ingrained in every individual; we are compelled to want to be the best versions of ourselves. Being successful in life is about being the person you want to be. You can only become the person you want to be by using things, and you can only use them freely once you have enough money to purchase them. Therefore, the most important understanding of all is to comprehend the science of becoming wealthy.

The desire to get wealthy is perfectly acceptable. It is admirable that people aspire to a greater, more plentiful existence, which is what is really meant by the desire for wealth. It is unnatural for a guy to not want to live a more rich life, and it is also abnormal for a man to not want enough money to acquire all he wants.

Our existence is driven by three primary desires: our physical needs, our mental needs, and our spiritual needs. None of them is superior to the others; they are all equally desired, and none of the three—body, intellect, or soul—can exist to its full potential if another is deprived of the opportunity to express itself completely. Living only for the soul while denying the mind and body is not honorable nor proper, nor is it acceptable to live for the intellect while denying the body and soul.

Real life, as we all know, is the full expression of all that man is capable of expressing via his body, mind, and soul. We are all familiar with the abhorrent results of living for the body and denying both mind and soul. Regardless of what he may say, a man cannot really be happy or fulfilled until his body is experiencing full vitality and his mind and soul are also experiencing full vitality. There is unfulfilled desire whenever there is an unspoken potential or an unfulfilled function. Desire is the manifestation of potential seeking performance, or function seeking expression.

A person cannot completely exist in the body without access to healthy food, cozy clothes, a warm place to dwell, and freedom from excessive labor. His physical well-being also depends on relaxation and leisure time.

Without books and the leisure to study them, without the chance to travel and observe, or without intellectual company, he cannot live completely in his head. In order to completely inhabit his mind, he has to engage in intellectual pursuits and surround himself with as many works of art and beauty as he is able to use and appreciate.

Man needs love to exist completely in the soul, and poverty prevents love from finding expression.

Giving to those you love is the greatest way for a man to discover pleasure since it is the most natural and spontaneous way for love to manifest itself. A guy who lacks anything can't be a good spouse or parent, a good citizen, or a good man. It is in the employment of material things that man finds complete life for his body, develops his intellect, and reveals his soul. Therefore, he considers it very essential that he be wealthy.

It is very OK for you to aspire to wealth; as a normal man or woman, you cannot help but feel this way. It is very appropriate that you focus your attention on the Science of Getting Rich, since it is the most important and honorable subject to study. You owe it to God, mankind, and yourself to take care of this study; there is no better service you can do for God and humanity than to maximize your own potential.

CHAPTER 2:

Getting Rich Has A Science To It

Like algebra or mathematics, there is a precise science to being wealthy. A guy may become wealthy with mathematical certainty if he learns and follows the rules that regulate the process of obtaining wealth.

Doing things in a specific manner results in the possession of money and property; those who follow this certain path, intentionally or unintentionally, become wealthy, while others who follow this another one, regardless of their ability or hard work, stay impoverished. Because of the natural rule that states similar causes always result in like outcomes, anybody who learns to do things in this particular manner will undoubtedly become wealthy. The following facts demonstrate the veracity of the preceding statement:—

Becoming wealthy is not influenced by one's surroundings, as this would lead to everyone in a neighborhood becoming wealthy, everyone in a city becoming wealthy while everyone else becomes poor, or everyone in one state becoming wealthy while everyone in a neighboring state becomes impoverished.

However, we constantly see wealthy and impoverished people coexisting in the same spaces, with similar occupations, and living side by side. It demonstrates that being wealthy is not largely influenced by one's surroundings when two guys in the same industry and neighborhood see one become wealthy while the other stays in poverty. While certain situations may be more conducive than others, if two guys in the same area and in the same business one succeeds while the other fails, it suggests that there is a certain way that one does things that leads to success.

Furthermore, skill alone does not always translate into the capacity to execute things in a certain way; many talented individuals struggle to make ends meet while others with far less talent succeed financially. Examining the wealthy, we see that they are a normal group of individuals with no exceptional skills or aptitudes compared to other males. It is clear that they get wealthy because they happen to do things a certain way rather than because they have special skills and abilities that other guys do not.

Rich individuals don't always end up that way because they save a lot of money or are "thrifts"; in fact, those who spend freely often end up wealthy.

Nor is being wealthy a result of accomplishing things that other people fail to do; for example, two individuals in the same firm often carry out almost identical tasks, with one of them becoming wealthy while the other stays in poverty or declares bankruptcy. Taking everything into consideration, we have to conclude that achieving wealth is the product of following a certain path. If achieving wealth is the outcome of following a certain path, and if similar causes always result in similar outcomes, then everyone who can follow that path may become wealthy, and the whole issue falls inside the purview of precise science.

Here, the issue of whether this Particular Way would not be so challenging that only a select few might pursue it emerges. As we have shown, in terms of inherent ability, this cannot be true. Rich people are made of talent, idiots are made of blockheads, great minds are made of extremely dumb people, physically strong individuals are made of money, and sick and frail people are made of money.

Naturally, a certain level of cognitive capacity is necessary; yet, in terms of innate aptitude, any anyone with sufficient common sense to read and comprehend these lines has the potential to become wealthy. We've also observed that environment has no bearing on it. Location is important; one would not expect to do a business in the middle of the Sahara.

Being wealthy requires you to interact with guys and be in a social environment; the more advantageous it is if the individuals you interact with have the same dealing style as you.

However, it is the extent of the environment. It is possible for you to become wealthy if it is possible for someone else in your town or state to do the same.

Once again, it has nothing to do with picking a certain industry or line of work. Individuals get wealthy in all businesses and professions, yet their next-door neighbors who practice the same trade continue to live in poverty. It is true that you will perform best in a company that you like and find agreeable; moreover, if you possess certain well-developed abilities, you will perform best in a firm that allows you to use them.

A company that is appropriate for your area will also provide the greatest results; for example, an ice cream shop would do better in a warm environment than in Greenland, and a salmon fishery would perform better in the Northwest than in Florida, where salmon are nonexistent.

Aside from these broad restrictions, however, being wealthy is more a result of knowing how to do things a certain way than it is of starting a certain firm. If you are in business and someone else in your community is making a lot of money from the same venture and you are not, it is likely because you are not carrying out your company operations in the same manner.

Lack of money never stops anybody from becoming wealthy. It's true that growth is easier and faster when you have money, but someone with capital is already wealthy and doesn't need to think about how to become richer. No matter how impoverished you are, if you start doing things a certain way, you will start to accumulate wealth and cash. Obtaining capital is a step in the process of becoming wealthy, and it is a component of the outcome that always follows doing things a certain way.

It doesn't matter whether you are the poorest guy on the continent, heavily in debt, without money, friends, or influence—if you start acting in this way, you will undoubtedly start becoming wealthy since similar causes inevitably lead to similar results. If you lack capital, you can acquire it; if you are in the wrong industry, you can enter the right industry; if you are in the wrong place, you can move to the right place; and you can accomplish all of this by starting in your current industry and location and carrying out actions in a certain way that leads to success.

CHAPTER 3:

Do Opportunities Get Monopolized?

No individual remains impoverished because opportunities have been denied to him or because money has been monopolized and fenced off by others. While you may not be able to do business via certain channels, you can still use others. Gaining control of any of the major train networks will likely be difficult for you since that industry is essentially monopolized. However, the electric railway industry is still very young and has a lot of room for growth. In a few short years, air traffic and transportation will grow into a major industry that employs hundreds of thousands, if not millions, of people in all of its branches. Instead of vying for a spot in the steam train industry with J. J.

Hill and others, why not focus on the advancement of aerial transportation?

It is true that there is very little chance for a worker employed by the steel trust to own the plant where they work; however, it is also true that if you start acting in a certain way, you can leave the steel trust's employ very quickly and purchase a farm of ten to forty acres to start a food production business. Men who live on little plots of land and farm them intensely have a lot of possibility right now; they will undoubtedly become wealthy. You may claim that it is impossible for you to get the property, but I will show you that it is not, and that if you work hard in a specific way, you can undoubtedly acquire a farm.

The requirements of the Whole and the specific stage of social development that has been attained determine which directions the tide of opportunity sets at various times. In America right now, the focus is on agriculture and related fields and occupations. The farmer in his line has more opportunities available to him now than the manufacturing worker has. It is available to both the businessman who supplies the farmer more so than the industrial worker and the professional guy who tends to the farmer more so than the working class person.

For the guy who would ride the tide rather than attempt to swim against it, opportunities abound.

Thus, neither as a class nor as individuals are the manufacturing workers denied opportunities. The masters are not "keeping down" the workers, nor are trusts and capital combinations "grounding" them. They are where they are as a class because they don't follow certain procedures. The American workers had the option to emulate their European counterparts by establishing large department stores and cooperative industries. They could also elect members of their own class to public office and enact laws that would encourage the growth of these cooperative industries. Eventually, they could peacefully seize control of the industrial sector.

When the working class starts acting in a certain way, they have the potential to rise to the status of the master class since everyone is subject to the same laws of wealth. They have to understand this, and as long as they keep acting in the same way, they will stay in their current position. The ignorance and mental laziness of his class, however, cannot hold down the individual worker; this book will show him how to ride the wave of opportunity to financial success.

A lack of wealth cannot keep someone in poverty; there is more than enough for everyone. With the building materials found in the United States alone, an entire family could have a palace the size of the capitol building in Washington. Additionally, with intensive cultivation, this nation would yield enough wool, cotton, linen, and silk to clothe every person on the planet in clothing more exquisite than that worn by Solomon in all of his glory, as well as enough food to feed them all in luxury. The supply that is visible is essentially limitless, whereas the supply that is unseen is really boundless.

There is just one initial element from which everything on earth is formed. Older forms dissolve and are always being replaced, yet One Thing assumes all forms.

The amount of Original Substance, or Formless Stuff, is infinite. It is the stuff that the cosmos is comprised of, although not all of it was used in its creation. The Original Substance, also known as the Formless Stuff or the basic substance of all things, is pervasive and fills in the voids within, through, and between the forms of the visible cosmos. Even when we have produced ten thousand times as much as we have, the supply of universal basic materials should not have run out. Therefore, no one is impoverished because of the state of nature or because there is insufficient for everyone.

There is never a shortage of wealth in nature as it is an endless source. With boundless creative force, Original Substance is always generating new forms. additional construction material will be created when the existing supply runs out; likewise, additional soil will be created or refreshed when it becomes too small to support the growth of food and clothes. More will be made from the Formless after all the gold and silver have been extracted from the ground, assuming that humankind is still at a point in its social evolution where gold and silver are necessary. Man's wants are met by the Formless Stuff, which ensures that he never goes without anything good.

This is true of man as a whole; the race is always very wealthy, and if any person is impoverished, it is because they do not adhere to the particular style of doing things that makes each individual wealthy. The Formless Stuff thinks; it is an intelligent substance. It is living and always drawn toward greater life. Life has an innate and natural desire to live longer; intellect and awareness both have a natural want to grow and discover more expansive ways to express themselves. Formless Living Substance, which threw itself into form to express itself more completely, created the world of forms.

The cosmos is a vast Living Presence that is always gravitating toward greater life and more complete functioning. The purpose of nature is to promote life; it is driven by the desire to do so. Everything that might possibly be needed to sustain life is abundantly given for this reason; there can be no shortage unless God were to contradict himself and undo his own creations. You are not kept impoverished by a lack of wealth; in fact, as I will show you a little later on, even the resources of the Formless Supply are within the reach of the person who chooses to behave and think in a certain way.

CHAPTER 4:

The First Rule In The Science Of Getting Rich.

The only force that can extract material wealth from the Formless Substance is thought. All things are composed of a material that has thinking, and it is this substance that generates form via the idea of form.

Every shape and activity you see in nature is the apparent manifestation of a thought in Original Substance, which moves in accordance with its ideas. The Formless Stuff takes on forms as it thinks of them and creates motions based on the forms it thinks of. Everything was made in this manner. Part of the thought universe is the thought world in which we dwell.

The idea of a moving cosmos permeated Formless Substance, and the Thinking Stuff that moved in accordance with that idea assumed the shape of planet systems and continued to do so. Thinking Substance moves in accordance with its thoughts, taking on the shape of its thoughts. It assumes the shape of these bodies, moving them as it thinks, carrying the notion of a circular system of suns and planets.

It moves in a manner akin to that of a slow-growing oak tree, even if it may take millennia to complete the task. When the Formless creates, it seems to follow the paths it has already created. For example, seeing an oak tree does not instantly result in the development of a fully realized tree, but it does initiate the forces necessary to construct the tree along predetermined growth paths. When one thinks about substance, every notion of form leads to the formation of that form, but usually speaking, those lines of growth and activity are already set.

If the idea of a particular kind of house were imprinted on Formless Substance, it might not result in the creation of the house right away, but it would direct creative energies already employed in trade and commerce in ways that would expedite the building of the house. Furthermore, the home would develop immediately from primordial essence without having to wait for the sluggish processes of the biological and inorganic universe, provided that there were no established channels through which the creative force might operate.

Original Substance cannot be imbued with any notion of form without first triggering the genesis of the form. Man is a thinking being with the capacity to generate thought. Before a man can shape anything with his hands, it must first exist in his mind; he cannot make something without first thinking it. Moreover, man has limited his endeavors to the work of his hands so far; he has used manual labor to alter or transform the universe of forms that already exist. He has never thought of attempting to influence the emergence of new forms by impressing his ideas onto Formless Substance.

When a man has a thought form, he constructs a picture of the form in his mind using elements from natural forms. He hasn't done much, if anything, to collaborate "with the Father"—that is, with Formless Intelligence—yet. The idea that he can "do what he seeth the Father doing" is not one of his dreams. Man uses physical work to reshape and modify forms that already exist; he hasn't thought of the possibility of producing things from Formless Substance by transmitting his ideas to it. Our proposal is to demonstrate that he is capable of doing so, as well as how any man or woman can accomplish so. First things first, there are three basic assumptions that need to be established.

Firstly, we claim that everything is formed from a single initial formless essence. Every apparently diverse element is really just one element presented in a different way; every variety of forms observed in both biological and inorganic nature are actually just variations on a single shape composed of the same material. Furthermore, this material is thought material; a concept contained inside it takes on its shape. Shapes are produced by thinking stuff via thought. Because man is an original thinker and a thinking center, he has the power to create the things he thinks about by communicating his thoughts to original thinking substances. In summary, this:—

All things are formed of a thinking substance that, in its primordial form, fills the voids in the cosmos and pervades everything. In this material, a mind generates the object it is seeing. Man has the ability to shape things in his mind and can bring about the creation of those forms by imprinting his thoughts into formless matter. whether someone were to ask whether I could provide evidence for these claims, I would say that I can, using both experience and reason, without getting into specifics.

I arrive at a single original thinking material by reasoning backward from the phenomena of form and thought. From this thinking substance, I go forward to the ability of man to create the production of the item he thinks about. I also found the rationale to be valid via experimentation, and this is my best evidence.

If a single guy who reads this book follows the advice and becomes wealthy, it proves my point; but, if every man who follows the advice succeeds in becoming wealthy is positive evidence that is, until someone tries the advice and fails. The notion holds true up until the process breaks down, but it won't since every guy who follows this book's instructions to the letter will become wealthy.

I have maintained that men get wealthy by acting in a specific manner, and that men must have a certain style of thinking in order to act in that way. The way a guy thinks about things directly influences the way he acts. The first step to being wealthy is learning how to think the way you want to think in order to accomplish tasks the way you want to. Regardless of appearances, thinking what you want to believe is the same as thinking the TRUTH.

Though it takes considerably more work to think what one wants to think than it does to think what appearances indicate, every individual has the innate and natural ability to think anything he wants to believe. Thinking based on appearances is simple; thinking based on truth, independent of appearances, is difficult and demands more energy than any other task a man must do.

The toughest effort in the world is continuous and sequential contemplation, and most individuals shun this kind of labor more than any other. This is particularly true when appearances don't match the reality. Every sight in the outside world seeks to elicit a comparable shape in the mind of the observer; the only way to stop this is to maintain the belief in the TRUTH.

If you do not believe in the fact that there is no such thing as sickness—that it is only an appearance and that health is the true state— then seeing the appearance of disease will lead to the form of disease in your own mind and, eventually, in your body.

If you believe that there is poverty but simply plenty, then looking at the outside manifestations of poverty will create comparable forms in your own mind.

It takes strength to think wealthy when everything around you seem poor, or to believe healthy while everything around you seems sick; yet the one who has this capacity is a MASTER MIND. He has the power to overcome destiny and achieve his goals.

The only way to get this ability is to grasp the fundamental truth that underlies all appearances, which is that there is only one Thinking Substance that serves as the basis and means for the creation of everything. Then we have to understand that every concept contained in this material takes on a shape, and that man may imprint his thoughts into it in such a way that they manifest as tangible objects.

When we come to this realization, we are free of any uncertainty and worry because we know that we have the ability to create the things we want, acquire the things we want, and develop into the people we want to be. The first step to becoming wealthy is to accept the three core ideas that were previously presented in this chapter. I will restate them again for emphasis:—

All things are formed of a thinking substance that, in its primordial form, fills the voids in the cosmos and pervades everything.

In this material, a mind generates the object it is seeing.

Man has the ability to shape things in his mind and can bring about the creation of those forms by imprinting his thoughts into formless matter.

You have to set aside all other conceptions of the cosmos and focus just on this monistic one until it becomes ingrained in your thoughts and habitual thinking. Reread these creeds many times, commit each word to memory, and consider them until you really believe what they say. If a doubt occurs to you, disregard it as a transgression. Avoid hearing arguments opposing this notion and avoid attending lectures or churches where a different viewpoint is taught or preached. Avoid reading books or periodicals that promote opposing viewpoints since doing so will only cause you to lose your faith.

Take these statements at face value without questioning their veracity or trying to figure out how they may be true. The complete embrace of this belief is the first step in the science of becoming wealthy.

CHAPTER 5:

Increasing Life.

The last shred of the antiquated notion that there is a Deity whose intention it is for you to be impoverished, or whose goals may be achieved by keeping you impoverished, must be banished.

A consciously living substance is the Intelligent Substance that is All, and in All, and that lives in All and in you. Given that it is a deliberately alive material, it must possess the innate and natural drive for more life, shared by all living intelligences. All organisms are in a constant state of search for ways to become larger, since life itself expands just by existing.

When a seed is planted in the earth, it immediately becomes active and multiplies by producing one hundred more seeds as it grows; this is how life multiplies. It is always Becoming More; if it stays at all, it has to do so.

The need for intelligence to continuously improve is the same. Because awareness is always growing, every idea we have requires us to think another notion. Knowledge never stops growing; each truth we discover drives us to discover another. We are prone to the impulse of life, seeking expression, which always pushes us to know more, do more, and be more. Every skill we develop inspires us to grow another talent.

We need more in order to know more, do more, and be more; we need things to use since we can only learn, act, and become via utilizing things. In order to live longer, we need to get wealthy. The pursuit of wealth is only the ability to live a more fulfilling life; all desires are the manifestation of an unspoken potential. yearning stems from the yearning for power to express itself. The same force that drives a plant to flourish is also responsible for your desire for more money; it's life, yearning for more complete manifestation.

The One Living Substance is compelled to create things because it is infused with the desire to live longer and is thus susceptible to this intrinsic rule of all life.

The One Substance wants all you can possibly need because it wants to be a bigger part of you.

God wants you wealthy. That is what He desires. He wants you to become wealthy because if you have a lot of resources at your disposal, you will be able to express yourself more effectively. If you have complete control over life's resources, then he may dwell more fully inside you.

- Everything you want is what the universe wants for you.
- Nature will cooperate with your intentions.
- For you, everything comes naturally.
- Decide for yourself that this is accurate.

Nonetheless, it is imperative that your mission align with the purpose of All. You have to be really interested in life, not only in sensory pleasures. Life is the execution of function; a person is only really alive when he fulfills all of his bodily, mental, and spiritual capacities without going above and beyond in any one of them.

You don't want to get wealthy in order to live a swinish lifestyle and satisfy your animal cravings—that is not what life is all about. However, carrying out all bodily functions is a necessary component of existence, and no one can really exist if they refuse to give their body's impulses a proper, healthy outlet.

You don't want to get wealthy only for intellectual fulfillment, to learn new things, to satisfy your ambition, to dominate people, or to become well-known. While all of these things have their place in life, a man who pursues his joys only via thought would only live half of his life and never be content with it.

You do not want to grow wealthy purely for the welfare of others, to lose oneself for the redemption of humanity, to feel the delights of generosity and sacrifice. Soul's delights are only a portion of existence; they are neither superior nor more honorable than any other portion.

You want to become wealthy so that you can see far-off places, feed your mind, grow intellectually, and be able to enjoy food, drink, and joy when the time comes. You also want to be wealthy so that you can surround yourself with beautiful things, love and be kind to others, and be able to contribute to the global search for truth.

But keep in mind that both excessive selfishness and extreme altruism are errors; none is superior nor nobler. Let go of the notion that you may win God's favor by giving up your own needs in order to benefit others; God doesn't need any such thing. He wants you to maximize your potential for both yourself and other people. There is no greater method to serve others than via optimizing your own potential. The only way you can fully express yourself is via money accumulation, thus it is appropriate and admirable that you should dedicate your whole attention to this endeavor.

But keep in mind that Substance's desire is for everyone, and that all of its actions must be directed toward giving everyone more life; it cannot be forced to work toward giving anybody less life since it seeks life and wealth equally from everyone. Though it won't take things away from someone else and give them to you, Intelligent Substance will produce things for you. You have to let go of the idea of rivalry. Your job is to produce, not to take up other people's work.

Nothing has to be taken away from anybody by you.
You're not required to drive a mean car.
It is not necessary for you to take advantage of or cheat. No individual should be forced to labor for you for less money than he is paid.
You don't need to be envious of other people's possessions or see them with hopelessness; nothing that a man has is beyond your reach, and you may have it without taking anything away from him.

You are to become a creator, not a rival; you will achieve your goals, but in a manner that will leave every other guy with less than he now has.

I should clarify that I am aware of some guys who make large sums of money by acting in direct contravention to the claims made in the previous paragraph. Those who belong to the plutocratic class and become very wealthy do so in two ways: either by sheer talent in the competitive arena, or by unintentionally aligning themselves with Substance's lofty goals and initiatives for the advancement of race via industrial development.

In the process of systematizing and organizing productive industry, individuals like as Rockefeller, Carnegie, Morgan, and others have acted as the Supreme's unwitting agents. Their efforts will ultimately greatly enhance the quality of life for everyone. Their time is almost over; they have set up production, and the agents of the crowd, who will set up the distribution apparatus shortly after, will take over.

Like the monstrous reptiles of ancient times, multimillionaires are an essential component of development, but the Power that created them will eventually eliminate them. It is also important to remember that they have never been really wealthy; an examination of the private affairs of the majority of this class will demonstrate that they have actually been the poorest and most destitute.

Wealth acquired via competition is never sufficient or long-lasting; it belongs to you today and to someone else tomorrow. Recall that you must completely break free from competitive thinking if you want to get wealthy in a methodical and scientific manner. Never, ever consider that there is a finite supply. You will temporarily lose your ability to create anything new when you start to believe that bankers and other powerful people are controlling all the money, that you must work hard to pass laws to stop this process, and other similar ideas. Worse yet, you may even put an end to the creative movements you have already started.

Know that there are untold millions of dollars' worth of gold hidden away in the earth's mountains, waiting to be discovered; if not, know that more would be produced from Thinking Substance to meet your demands.

YOU MUST KNOW that you will get the money you need, even if it takes a thousand men to find fresh gold mines tomorrow.

Never look at the apparent supply; instead, focus only on the boundless wealth found in Formless Substance, and KNOW that it will come to you as quickly as it can be used and received. Nobody can deny you what is rightfully yours by seizing the obvious supply.

Therefore, unless you're in a rush, never allow yourself to believe that all of the prime construction lots will be gone before you start constructing your home. Never be concerned about trusts and combines, and get nervous because you think they'll soon take over the whole planet. Never let the fear of someone else "beating you to it" prevent you from pursuing your goals. That is not possible; you are creating what you want from Formless Substance, and there is an infinite supply; you are not looking for something that someone else has. Adhere to the following formulation:—

All things are formed of a thinking substance that, in its primordial form, fills the voids in the cosmos and pervades everything. In this material, a mind generates the object it is seeing. Man has the ability to shape things in his mind and can bring about the creation of those forms by imprinting his thoughts into formless matter.

CHAPTER 6:

How Riches Come To You.

It is important to note that I am not saying that you do not have to drive sharp bargains or that you are exempt from the need to engage in transactions with other people. That is to say, you won't have to treat people unjustly; instead of expecting something in exchange for nothing, you may offer each guy more than you take from him.

You can't offer a guy more in use value than the financial worth of what you take from him, but you may give him more in market value than what you take from him. This book may not be worth the money you spent for the paper, ink, and other materials it contains, but if the ideas it offers help you make thousands of dollars, the people who sold it to you were not incorrect;

they gave you a valuable tool for a negligible amount of money.

Assume for the moment that I possess a painting by a renowned artist, which is valued thousands of dollars in any civilized society. I take it to Baffin Bay and, using "salesmanship," I get an Eskimo to trade it for a $500 bundle of furs. I have really harmed him because he doesn't appreciate the photo and it won't make a difference in his life. However, if I offer him a $50 rifle in exchange for his furs, he's struck a decent deal. He can use the rifle; it will let him get a lot more food and furs; it will improve every aspect of his life; and it will make him wealthy.

As you transition from a competitive to a creative plane, you will be able to closely examine every commercial transaction you do. If you find that you are selling a guy something that does not improve his life more than what he provides you in return, you can afford to quit. In business, you don't have to outperform everyone. And leave your company right away if it involves beating individuals. Every economic transaction you engage in adds to the life of the planet if you give every guy more in terms of use value than you take from him in terms of financial worth.

If you have employees, you have to pay them less in salary than you obtain from them in financial value. However, you may set up your company to promote progression and allow any person who wants to do so to make a little progress each day. What this book is doing for you, you can make your company do for your staff. You may handle your company that it will be a type of ladder, by which every employee who will take the effort may climb to riches himself; and given the chance, if he will not do so it is not your responsibility.

Lastly, it does not follow that your riches must materialize out of thin air and appear before your own eyes, because you are to be the agents of their production from the Formless Substance that penetrates every part of your surroundings.

For example, if you want a sewing machine, I do not intend to suggest that you must imprint the image of a sewing machine on Thinking

Substance until the machine is created in the space where you are sitting, or in another location, without the need for hands. However, if you have your heart set on a sewing machine, visualize it with the utmost confidence that it is either being manufactured or is its route to you. Once the idea has been formed, have the utmost confidence and lack of doubt that the sewing machine will come; never discuss or think about it in any other manner than as something that is certain to happen. Declare it to be yours already.

It will come to you via the influence of the Almighty Intelligence on human thought processes. If you reside in Maine, there's a chance a guy from Texas or Japan may be brought in to do some kind of deal that will get you what you want. If that is the case, that guy stands to gain just as much from the situation as you do.

Remember always that the Thinking Substance is through everything, in everything, speaking with everything, and having the power to affect everything. All sewing machines now in production are the result of Thinking

Substance's desire for a better life and a more fulfilling existence. When men behave in a certain way and with faith and desire, they have the power to create millions more sewing machines. It is undoubtedly possible for you to own a sewing machine in your home, and it is equally likely that you can own any other item or items that you like and will use to improve both your own and other people's lives.

In general, you don't need to be afraid to ask; Jesus stated, "It is your Father's pleasure to give you the kingdom."

Original Substance desires for you to have all you may possibly need to live the fullest, most abundant existence imaginable. Your faith becomes unbreakable if you focus on the awareness that your desire for wealth is a combination of your desire for Omnipotence to manifest itself more fully.

I once saw a little child sitting at a piano, futilely attempting to produce harmony with the keys; it was evident to me that he was distressed and agitated by his incapacity to produce authentic music. "I can feel the music in me, but

I can't make my hands go right," he said when I asked him what was bothering him. All of music was seeking expression via the kid; it was the URGE of Original Substance, which contained all of life's potential.

Through humans, God, the One Substance, tries to live, act, and enjoy life. He is expressing himself in this way: "I want feet to run my errands, eyes to see my beauties, tongues to tell mighty truths and to sing marvelous songs; I want hands to build wonderful structures, to play divine harmonies, to paint glorious pictures," and so on.

All that is possible is trying to find expression in men. God wants people who can play music to have access to pianos and other instruments, as well as the means to fully develop their talents; He wants people who can appreciate beauty to be surrounded by beautiful things; He wants people who can discern truth to have access to as many opportunities for travel and observation as possible; He wants people who can appreciate fashion to be exquisitely dressed; and He wants people who can appreciate fine food to be lavishly fed.

He desires all of these things because He is the one who values and enjoys them; God is the one who wants to sing, perform, enjoy beauty, declare the truth, dress elegantly, and eat delectable delicacies. "It is God that worketh in you to will and to do," declared Paul. Your desire for wealth is the Infinite's attempt to express Himself in you, just as He did with the little child playing the piano. Therefore, don't be afraid to ask big questions. It is your responsibility to emphasize and communicate God's will.

Most people find this difficult to accept because they still harbor the antiquated belief that selflessness and poverty are acceptable to God. They consider poverty to be a natural need and a component of the scheme. They believe that God has created all that He is capable of creating, that the bulk of people must remain in poverty because there isn't enough for everyone, and that God has completed His job. They attempt not to seek more than a very little competence, just enough to keep them quite comfortable, since they adhere to this false belief so strongly that they feel embarrassed to ask for riches.

I can still clearly remember the instance of a student who was instructed to visualize his goals in order to imprint his original ideas into Formless Substance. He was a very poor guy who only had what he earned on a daily basis, lived in a leased home, and was unable to understand that all riches belonged to him. After giving it some thought, he concluded that he might justifiably request an anthracite coal burner to heat the home in the winter and a new rug for the floor of his finest room. After a few months of following the directions in this book, he acquired these things; and then it occurred to him that he had not asked for enough. He inspected his home and made a list of all the upgrades he wanted to make; he imagined adding a bay window here, a room there, until his perfect house was complete. He then planned the furnishings for his new home.

With the whole vision in his head, he started living the Certain Way and making progress toward his goals. He now owns the home and is restoring it to resemble his imagined version.

And he is now doing bigger things with an even greater faith. He has experienced everything in accordance with his beliefs, and the same is true for you and the rest of us.

CHAPTER 7:

Gratitude.

The reader will have understood from the pictures in the previous chapter that communicating your desires to the Formless Substance is the first step towards becoming wealthy. This is accurate, and you will discover that doing so necessitates a healthy relationship with the Formless Intelligence.

Maintaining this harmonic relationship is so important that I will explain it in some detail here and provide you with directions that, if you follow, will undoubtedly bring you into complete harmony with God. Gratitude is the key to the whole process of atonement and mental adjustment.

You link to the Intelligent Substance via a great sense of thankfulness. First, you think that there is only one Intelligent Substance from which all things originate. Secondly, you believe that this Substance fulfills all of your desires.

Those who lead morally upright lives in every other aspect are often held in poverty due to a lack of appreciation. After receiving one gift from God, they neglect to acknowledge Him, severing the connection between them. It is simple to comprehend that riches increases with our proximity to the source of prosperity. It is equally simple to comprehend that a grateful person maintains a stronger relationship with God than one who seldom expresses gratitude to Him.

When wonderful things happen to us, the more gratefully we focus our thoughts on the Supreme, the more and faster the good things occur. The reason for this is because having a thankful mental attitude brings the mind closer to the source of the benefits.

If the idea that being grateful puts your whole mind into greater harmony with the creative energy of the cosmos seems novel to you, give it some serious consideration and you'll find that it is accurate. The blessings you now enjoy have come your way as a result of following the law. Having gratitude will guide your thoughts to follow the paths that things take, maintain you in harmony with creative thinking, and prevents you from drifting into competitive thought.

Gratitude is the only thing that can keep your eyes on the All and protect you from making the deadly mistake of believing that there is a finite supply. If you want the outcomes you want, you have to follow the Law of Gratitude, which is vitally important.

The natural rule that action and response are always equal and go in different directions is known as the law of appreciation. A release or expenditure of power results from your glad thoughts reaching out in appreciative praise to the Supreme; it cannot fail to reach its intended recipient, and the response is an immediate movement toward you.

"Go closer to God, and He will come closer to you." That is a psychologically accurate statement.

And if you are really grateful, you will experience a powerful and ongoing response in Formless Substance, where the things you want will constantly come your way. Take note of Jesus' attitude of gratitude—he seemed to be repeating, "I thank Thee, Father, that Thou hearest me" constantly. Without appreciation, it is impossible to exert much power since gratitude is what maintains your connection to Power.

However, being grateful is not only about obtaining additional gifts down the road. Without thankfulness, it is impossible to resist thinking negatively about the state of affairs for very long. You start to lose ground as soon as you allow your thoughts to remain in discontent with things as they are. You focus on the mundane, the ordinary, the impoverished, the filthy and the mean; and these things become forms in your imagination. The common, the poor, the dirty, and the mean will come to you when you communicate these forms or mental pictures to the Formless.

Allowing your thoughts to focus on what is inadequate means that you will surround yourself with and become inferior. However, concentrating on the best means surrounding yourself with the best and improving yourself. We become the reflection of whatever we focus on because of the Creative Power that is inside us.

Thinking Substance is what we are, and thinking substance always assumes the shape of its thoughts. Because the thankful mind is always focused on the greatest, it tends to become the best, adopts the best characteristics, and will be showered with the best.

Moreover, appreciation is the seed of faith. The appreciative mind is full of expectations, and expectations grow into faith. Faith is created by the thankful mind responding with appreciation, and faith grows with each glad outpouring of thanksgiving. A person without thankfulness cannot sustain a live faith for very long. As we will see in the next chapters, you cannot become wealthy via the creative process without a living faith.

Therefore, it is essential to develop the practice of being thankful for everything that comes your way and to express your gratitude on a regular basis. You should express your thanks to everything since everything has helped you progress. Spend no time discussing or reflecting on the flaws or bad deeds of trust magnates or plutocrats. Your opportunities have been made possible by the way they have organized the world; everything you have really comes from them. Please do not get enraged with dishonest politicians; without them, chaos would reign and you would have far less opportunities.

God has slowly and over a long period of time brought us to this point in government and business, and He continues to do so. He will certainly remove politicians, trust magnates, plutocrats, and captains of business as soon as He can, but in the meanwhile, observe that they are all excellent. Recall that they are all involved in setting up the channels of transmission by which your wealth will arrive, and extend your gratitude to each and every one of them. By doing this, you will establish harmonious relationships with everything that is good, and all that is good will gravitate toward you.

CHAPTER 8:

Thinking In The Certain Way.

You will have a decent understanding of the first step toward being wealthy if you go back to chapter 6 and read the account of the guy who saw his home in his mind. You cannot communicate an idea unless you own it yourself, therefore you must visualize what you desire clearly and firmly in your mind. Before you can offer it, you must first have it. This is why many individuals fall short of impressing Thinking Substance because they only have a hazy idea of what it is they want to do, own, or become.

The mere desire to obtain riches "to do good with" is insufficient; everyone has such goal.

It is insufficient to just want to travel, see new things, live a longer life, etc.

These are wants that are shared by everybody. When sending a wireless message to a buddy, you wouldn't just give him the alphabet's letters in the right sequence and let him put the message together on his own, nor would you choose words at random from a dictionary. You would send a meaningful statement that made sense. Remember that you need to make your desires clear to Substance by making a well-reasoned statement. You also need to be specific about what you want.

Sending out nebulous wants and unformed longings will never lead to wealth or ignite the creative force. Examine your aspirations in the same manner as the guy I've mentioned did with his home; choose exactly what you want and see it in your mind's eye as you would want it to appear when it becomes yours. You have to maintain your face pointed in the direction of that distinct mental image at all times, much like a sailor does when he is sailing his ship. It is imperative that you don't lose sight of it any more than a steersman does of the compass.

It is not required to do concentration exercises, schedule specific periods for prayer and affirmation, "go into the silence," or engage in any form of occult practices. These elements are sufficient; all you really need is to know what you want and to want it intensely enough for it to occupy your mind.

Take as much time as you can to think about your image during your free time. The things you don't really care about are the ones that demand work to focus your attention on. Nobody has to do exercises to focus their thoughts on something they really desire. It won't be worth it for you to attempt to follow the directions in this book unless you really want to become wealthy, to the point where the desire is strong enough to keep your thoughts focused on the goal as the magnetic pole holding the compass needle.

The strategies presented here are meant for those whose need for wealth is great enough to push beyond mental sloth and a preference for comfort and successfully implement them. Your want will thus be greater the clearer and more specific your vision is, and the more you focus on it, highlighting all of its exquisite features; the stronger your desire, the simpler it will be to keep your attention focused on the picture of what you want.

But seeing the image clearly is not enough. More is required. If that's all you do, you're just a dreamer with little to no ability to make things happen. Your distinct vision must have a goal to be realized, to be brought to life in a practical way. And underneath this goal has to be an unyielding and unstoppable FAITH that the item is already yours, that it is "at hand," and all you need to do is grab hold of it. Until the new home materializes around you, live there in your mind. Go right now into the mental space and experience anything that you want.

Jesus stated, "Believe that you will receive whatever you ask for in prayer, and you will have it."

Imagine yourself possessing and using the things you want as if they were indeed always there. Use your imagination with them, just as you would with actual material goods. Focus on your mental image until it is definite and clear, and then approach everything in that image with the Mental Attitude of Ownership. Remember to take control of it with the whole belief that it is really yours. Maintain this mental possession; do not even for a moment falter in your belief that it is true.

And keep in mind the thankfulness advice from the previous chapter; continuously express your thanks for it to the extent that you anticipate doing so after it has taken shape. A man has true faith when he can honestly give thanks to God for the things he can only imagine owning up to now. He will become wealthy and bring about the production of everything he desires. It's not essential to inform God about your desires every day or to pray for them constantly.

Jesus told His students, "Your Father knows that you have need of these things before you ask Him. Use not vain repetitions as the heathens do."

It is your responsibility to carefully consider what you would want out of life and organize your desires into a cohesive whole. Then, you must impress this Whole Desire onto the

Formless Substance, which has the will and ability to grant your wishes. You don't leave this effect by reciting words; rather, you leave an impression by hanging onto the goal with unwavering PURPOSE to achieve it and unwavering FAITH that you will succeed.

Your prayer will be answered in accordance with your working faith, not in accordance with your talking faith. You can't make an impression on God by telling Him what you want on a designated Sabbath day and then ignoring Him the rest of the week. If you set up certain times to pray in your closet and then forget about it until the next prayer hour, you won't be able to make an impression on Him.

spoken prayer is sufficient and may help you define your goals and improve your faith, particularly in relation to oneself. However, your spoken requests won't grant your wishes. You need to "pray without ceasing"—not a "sweet hour of prayer"—if you want to become wealthy. And by prayer, I mean clinging firmly to your vision and your trust that you are bringing it to pass, in order to bring it into concrete shape. "Think that you are receiving them."

After you have a distinct vision, everything depends on receiving. Once you have formulated it, it is optimal to express yourself verbally, speaking to the Almighty in a respectful and prayerful manner; and from that point on, you must remember to accept your requests. Move into the new home, dress well, drive, go on the trip, and boldly make plans for longer travels. Consider and discuss all you have requested in terms of real, existing ownership.

Create an atmosphere and financial situation that you would want to live in, and then assume those conditions constantly. But keep in mind that you are not doing this out of a simple desire to construct a castle and dream; rather, you are doing this with the PURPOSE to actualize the imaginary and the FAITH that it is being realized. Recall that the difference between a scientist and a dreamer is their belief and intent while using their imagination. Now that you are aware of this reality, you need to understand how to use the Will correctly.

CHAPTER 9:

How To Apply The Will.

You don't attempt to use your willpower to achieve something external to yourself when you approach wealth creation in a scientific manner. In any case, you are not entitled to do so. Applying your will to other men and women to force them to do what you want is wrong.

Both using physical force and mental coercion to compel someone is blatantly immoral. If forcing someone to do tasks for you by physical force lowers them to slavery, then forcing someone to perform tasks for you mentally achieves the exact same result; the techniques are only different. There is no distinction in principle between robbery and stealing something from someone by physical or mental coercion if taking something from them by force is likewise considered theft.

Even "for his own good," you have no right to exert your willpower over someone else as you have no idea what is in their best interests. The science of wealth creation does not, in any kind, call for you to use force or authority over another individual. It is not at all necessary to do this; in fact, trying to force your will on other people will only serve to undermine your goals.

To force things to come to you, you do not need to apply your will to them. That would be silly, pointless, and disrespectful as it would amount to forcing God to do anything. Just like you don't need to exert your willpower to make the sun rise, you don't need to force God to give you wonderful things. It is not necessary to utilize your willpower to subdue an antagonistic god or to coerce obstinate and disobedient powers to comply with your wishes.

When it comes to giving you what you desire, substance is more eager to oblige you than you are to receive it. All you have to do to get wealthy is force your will onto yourself. Once you are aware of the proper thoughts and actions, you need to utilize your willpower to force yourself to act and think in the proper ways. This is a proper use of willpower to achieve your goals and keep yourself on the correct path. Make use of your willpower to maintain the Certain Way of thinking and behaving.

Avoid trying to "act" on objects or people by projecting your ideas, will, or mind into space. Keep your mind at home; it can do more there than elsewhere. Create a mental picture of what you desire in your mind, hang onto it with trust and purpose, and use your willpower to keep your mind focused in the correct direction. You will get wealthy more quickly if your faith and purpose are more constant and unwavering because you will only leave positive imprints on substance—negative impressions won't cancel one another out or balance each other out. For all I know, the Formless takes up your image of your wishes, held with trust and purpose, and spreads it over the cosmos, across tremendous distances.

As this impression grows, everything is geared toward realizing it; everything—animate and inanimate, as well as the entities that have not yet been created—is compelled to bring about the things that you want. Everything starts to move in your direction and all force starts to be applied. People's thoughts are affected to do the actions required to realize your wishes wherever you look, and they unwittingly work in your favor.

However, all of this may be verified by initiating a negative impression in the Formless Substance. Just as faith and purpose are sure to start a movement toward you, doubt and disbelief will undoubtedly start one away from you. The majority of individuals who attempt to employ "mental science" as a means of becoming wealthy fail because they fail to grasp this. Every hour and minute you waste in paying regard to doubts and concerns, every hour you spend in stress, every hour in which your soul is dominated by disbelief, sets a current away from you throughout the entire realm of intelligent Substance. Only those who believe are the recipients of all the promises.

Observe how adamant Jesus was about this idea, and you now understand why.

Because beliefs are everything, you should protect your thoughts. Since what you notice and think about can greatly influence your views, it's critical that you take control of your attention. Here is where the will is put to work because you choose what will capture your attention and focus it. You should not study poverty if your goal is to get wealthy.

One does not create things by contemplating their opposites. Studying and thinking about sickness will never bring about health; studying and thinking about sin will never bring about righteousness; and studying and thinking about poverty will never bring about wealth.

As a science of sickness, medicine has caused more illness; as a science of sin, religion has encouraged sin; and as a study of poverty, economics will cause more misery and lack in the world. Avoid discussing or looking at poverty, and don't worry about it. You have nothing to do with its causes, therefore don't worry about them. You're worried about the remedy.

Don't waste your time on charity activities or benevolent initiatives; they all have the tendency to prolong the misery they are meant to relieve. I'm not saying that you should ignore the cry of need or be callous, but you also shouldn't aim to end poverty in the traditional sense. Put poverty and everything related to it behind you, and then "make good." The greatest way to assist the impoverished is to become wealthy.

And if you surround yourself with images of poverty, you will find it difficult to maintain the mental image that will make you wealthy. Avoid reading publications or books that provide hints about the misery of tenement residents, the atrocities of child labor, and other such topics. Avoid reading anything that conjures up depressing pictures of pain and lack.

Knowing about these things won't benefit the impoverished in the slightest, and widespread awareness of them won't make poverty go away either. It is not images of poverty that tend to eradicate poverty; rather, it is images of prosperity imprinted in the brains of the impoverished.

When you refuse to let images of such suffering dominate your thoughts, you are not abandoning the poor in their pain. The only way to end poverty is not to increase the number of wealthy individuals who consider it, but rather to increase the number of impoverished individuals who really want to become wealthy.

The impoverished want inspiration more than alms. While charity only provides them with a loaf of bread to tide them over in their agony or an hour or two of amusement, inspiration is what will lift them out of their squalor. Help the impoverished by showing them that they can achieve wealth by becoming wealthy yourself.

Poverty will never be eradicated from our planet unless a sizable and steadily growing number of individuals put this book's lessons into practice. It is important to teach people that wealth is created, not acquired via rivalry. When a guy becomes wealthy via competition, he pulls down the ladder that helps him climb and discourages others from doing the same. However, when a man becomes wealthy through invention, he creates a path for thousands of others to follow and encourages them to do so.

When you refuse to feel sorry for poverty, observe poverty, read about poverty, think about poverty, speak about poverty, or listen to others who do talk about poverty, you are not displaying a hard heart or an insensitive nature. Use your willpower to focus your faith and purpose on the vision of what you desire, and to keep your thoughts off the topic of poverty.

CHAPTER 10:

Further Use Of The Will.

It is impossible to maintain a genuine and coherent understanding of riches if your focus is continually drawn to contradicting images, real or imagined. If you have had financial difficulties in the past, do not discuss them or even think about them. Never discuss your parents' poverty or the difficulties you had as a child. Doing so would subconsciously categorize you as impoverished for the time being and would undoubtedly impede the progress of events in your favor.

As Jesus stated, "Let the dead bury their dead."

Put poverty behind you, along with everything related to it. You've decided that a certain theory about the world is true, and you're basing all of your expectations for happiness on it. What good is it to pay attention to opposing theories? Avoid reading religious texts that predict the end of the world or the works of muckrakers and gloomy thinkers who claim the world is headed toward the devil. The world is not heading to the devil; it is going to God. It's an amazing Becoming.

It's true that there are probably a lot of unpleasant things about the current state of affairs; but what use is it to study them when they are undoubtedly dying and studying them tends merely to confirm their death and preserve them for us? If you can only expedite the elimination of things that are being eliminated by evolutionary development by supporting it to the extent that it affects you, then why devote time and energy to things that are being eliminated by it?

No matter how terrible the circumstances are in certain nations, regions, or locations, thinking about them will just squander your time and ruin your prospects. You need to put some effort into being wealthy. Consider the wealth the world is acquiring rather than the poverty it is emerging from, and remember that the only way you can help the world get wealthier is by becoming wealthy yourself via the creative, not the competitive, route.

Focus only on wealth; pay no attention to poverty. Every time you consider or discuss the impoverished, see them as individuals who are on the path to prosperity; individuals who deserve congratulations rather than sympathy. Subsequently, they and others will get inspired and start looking for a way out. It does not follow that you should be vile or cruel because I suggest that you should devote all of your time, attention, and thinking to acquiring wealth.

The highest goal one may pursue in life is to become very wealthy, since it encompasses all other goals. On a competitive level, pursuing wealth might be seen as a godless race to dominate others; yet, this is all altered when one enters the creative realm. Getting wealthy is the means by which grandeur and soul-unfoldment, service and high effort, are all made possible; everything is made possible via the use of things.

If you are not in good physical health, you will discover that getting well is dependent on your wealth. Health can only be attained and maintained by individuals who are freed from financial burden, have the wherewithal to live a carefree life, and practice good hygiene.

Only those who rise above the competitive struggle for life may achieve moral and spiritual grandeur, and only those who are getting wealthy on the plane of creative thinking are immune to the demeaning effects of competition. If your heart is bent on family bliss, keep in mind that love thrives in environments of refinement, high thinking, and freedom from corrupting influences; they are only found in environments where riches are acquired with the application of creative ideas, free from conflict or competition.

I'll say it again: there are no goals as magnificent or honorable as being wealthy. You have to focus only on your imagined wealth, ignoring everything that may cloud your view. You have to have the ability to discern the TRUTH underneath everything that seems to be wrong, and you must see the Great One Life always progressing in the direction of greater expression and overall pleasure.

It is a fact that riches exist alone and that poverty does not exist. Some individuals never realize they can be wealthy; you may best teach them this by demonstrating for them how to become wealthy in both your personal and professional life.

For others, the best thing you can do is to pique their desire by demonstrating the happiness that comes from being rightfully rich, even though they feel that there is a way out but are too intellectually lazy to put forth the mental effort required to find that way and travel it.

Some remain impoverished despite having some understanding of science because they are so overwhelmed and disoriented by the tangle of occult and metaphysical notions that they are unsure of which path to follow. They experiment with a variety of systems and ultimately fail. Again, the best course of action for these is to practice and model the proper behavior for others; an ounce of action is worth a pound of theory.

Making the most of who you are is the finest thing you can do for everyone on the planet. There is no more effective way to serve God and mankind than to become wealthy—that is, if you do it using creative means rather than competing ones.

Another thing. We claim that the concepts of the science of becoming wealthy are covered in full in this book, and if that is the case, you don't need to read any other books on the topic. While this may come out as limiting and conceited, keep in mind that there is no more scientific way to compute in mathematics than addition, subtraction, multiplication, and division. Between any two locations, there can only be one shortest path.

Thinking in a manner that takes the shortest and most straightforward path to the objective is the only way to approach science. No one has created a "system" that is shorter or less intricate than the one shown here; it has been pared down to the fundamentals. Set everything else aside and completely forget about it once you start working on this. Read this book every day, carry it around with you, memorize it, and avoid thinking about other "systems" or ideas. If you do, you'll start to question yourself and become unsure and erratic in your thinking, which will lead to mistakes.

Once you have achieved success and wealth, you are free to study other methods as much as you want. However, until you are certain that you have achieved your goals, stick to this book and nothing else on the subject, unless it is written by the writers listed in the Preface. And just peruse the global news remarks that are the most upbeat and consistent with your image. Also, postpone your research into the occult. Never experiment with spiritualism, theosophy, or related fields of study. The deceased are probably still alive and about, but if so, please leave them alone and take care of yourself.

The deceased have their own jobs to accomplish and issues to resolve, wherever they may be, and we have no right to get in the way of them. We are unable to assist them, and it is quite unlikely that they will be able to do so, nor that we have the right to intrude on their time even if they do. Leave the dead and the hereafter alone, take care of your own issues, and get wealthy. If you start interacting with the occult, you'll create mental rifts that will undoubtedly cause your aspirations to crash. We have now arrived at the following summary of fundamental facts thanks to this and the previous chapters:—

All things are formed of a thinking substance that, in its primordial form, fills the voids in the cosmos and pervades everything. In this material, a mind generates the object it is seeing. Man has the ability to shape things in his mind and can bring about the creation of those forms by imprinting his thoughts into formless matter.

Man must transform from a competitive to a creative mind in order to accomplish this. He must visualize what he wants and hold this image in his mind along with a resolute PURPOSE to achieve his goals and an unwavering FAITH that he will succeed. He must also close his mind to anything that could undermine his goals, cloud his vision, or stifle his faith. We will also see that he has to live and behave in a certain way on top of all of this.

CHAPTER 11:

Acting In The Certain Way.

Thought is the creative power, or the driving factor behind the creative power's actions; you may get wealthy by thinking a certain way, but you must not depend only on thought and ignore taking personal action. The inability to link cognition with action is the rock that many apparently scientific metaphysical philosophers crash and burn.

Even if such a degree of development were feasible, we have not yet arrived at it; man still has to complement his cognition with personal action in addition to thinking; he cannot create straight from Formless Substance without the aid of human hands or the processes of nature.

You have the ability to direct the gold that is inside the mountains towards you by thinking, but it won't come rolling down the roads, wanting to find its way into your pocket, or mine, refine, or coin itself into double eagles.

The Supreme Spirit will direct other men's business transactions in a way that will bring the gold to you, and you must direct your own business affairs in a way that will allow you to receive it when it comes to you. Men's affairs will be so ordered under this impelling power that someone will be led to mine the gold for you. Your thoughts cause everything, living or dead, to work toward your goals; yet, your actions must be such that you are able to appropriately accept your goals when they come your way. You are to offer every man more in use value than he provides you in financial worth; you are not to accept it as charity or steal it.

Forming a clear and definite mental picture of what you desire, keeping tight to the objective of getting it, and recognizing with glad trust that you do achieve it are the three components of the scientific use of thinking. Avoid attempting to "project" your thoughts in an esoteric or cryptic manner in the hopes of getting them to perform tasks for you; this will just make you less capable of thinking clearly and will be a waste of time.

The previous chapters provide a detailed explanation of the thought process involved in becoming wealthy. Your vision of Formless Substance, which shares your desire for more life, is positively influenced by your faith and purpose, and this vision, in turn, directs all creative forces toward you through their regular channels of action.

You just need to hold onto your vision, be true to your goal, and never waver in your faith and appreciation. There is no need for you to direct or oversee the creative process. However, you have to behave in a certain way in order to take possession of what is really yours; to view the items in your image and arrange them as they become available.

It's easy to see that this is true. Things will be in the hands of other men when they get to you, and they will demand an equivalent for them.

And by giving the other guy what is his, you can only get what is yours. Your wallet won't magically become into Fortunatus's purse, which will constantly be loaded with cash without any work on your part.

This is the critical juncture in the science of wealth accumulation, whereby the integration of human action and cognition is necessary. Many individuals, whether intentionally or unintentionally, activate the creative forces via the intensity and tenacity of their wishes, yet they continue to live in poverty as a result of their inability to make provisions for receiving their desired outcome when it materializes. The thing you want comes to you via thinking, and you get it via doing.

It is obvious that you must take action NOW, regardless of what that action may be. Since you are unable to change the past, it is imperative that you erase it from your memory in order to maintain mental clarity. The future is not here yet, therefore you cannot act in it. Furthermore, you can never predict how you will wish to respond until a future emergency arises.

Do not believe that you have to wait to take action until you find the perfect company or environment since you are not in either right now. Additionally, trust that you will be able to handle any situation that arises and avoid wasting time thinking about what to do in the future.

You will be acting with a split mind and ineffectively if you behave in the now while thinking about the future. Give the task at hand your whole attention. You will never obtain results if you give Original Substance your creative drive and then sit back and wait for it to happen. Take immediate action. There has never been a better moment than this one, and there never will be. You have to start now if you are ever going to start preparing yourself for receiving what you desire.

And whatever you decide to do, it will very certainly have to do with your current job or company and with the people and things in your immediate surroundings. You can only take action from where you are, not from where you have been, where you are going, or from where you are not.

Put today's work first and don't worry about how well or poorly yesterday's job was completed.

There will be plenty of time to do the task when you get to it, so don't attempt to do tomorrow's work today.

Avoid attempting to influence people or things that are beyond your control by occult or magical methods.

Act now to bring about a change in the environment rather than waiting for one. You have the power to influence your current surroundings in such a way that you are moved to a better one. While you should act with all of your heart, might, and intellect toward improving your current surroundings, hold onto your image of yourself in a better situation with faith and purpose.

Don't waste time daydreaming or constructing castles; stick to your one goal and take action right now.

Don't go looking for a novel activity to engage in, or a peculiar, uncommon, or noteworthy deed to carry out as a first step toward being wealthy. Your activities will most likely be the same as they have been for some time to come, at least for a while; nevertheless, you must start doing these acts right away in a certain way that will undoubtedly make you wealthy.

Do not wait to take action until you are in the correct business if you are already involved in one and feel that it is not the right one for you. Take action right now. You are lost, but don't give up or sit down and moan about it. No man ever got so lost but that he could find his way back home, and no man ever got so entangled in the wrong trade but that he could enter the correct trade.

Maintain the mental image of yourself in the ideal industry, determined to enter it and full of trust that you will and are doing so; yet, take action in your current industry. Make the most of your current business to acquire a better one, and make the most of your current surroundings to enter a better one. If your vision of the correct business is held with confidence and purpose, the Supreme will bring the right business to you; if you act in the Certain Way, the business will come to you.

Do not "project" your ideas into space and hope that doing so would get you a new job if you are an employee or wage earner and believe that you must relocate in order to achieve what you desire. It most likely won't be able to. You will undoubtedly get the job you desire if you have a clear picture of yourself in the role you want and act with trust and purpose in the one you now have. Your activity will trigger the forces in your own surroundings to propel you toward the destination you desire, and your vision and faith will unleash the creative energy to bring it nearer you.

We will conclude this chapter by adding a new item to our syllabus: there is a thinking substance that forms the basis of everything and that, in its primordial form, fills the gaps in the cosmos.

In this material, a mind generates the object it is seeing. Man has the ability to shape things in his mind and can bring about the creation of those forms by imprinting his ideas into formless matter.

Man must transform from a competitive to a creative mind in order to accomplish this. He must visualize what he wants and hold this image in his mind along with a resolute PURPOSE to achieve his goals and an unwavering FAITH that he will succeed. He must also close his mind to anything that could undermine his goals, cloud his vision, or stifle his faith. Man must take action NOW toward the people and things in his current surroundings in order to obtain what he desires when it arrives.

CHAPTER 12:

Efficient Action.

Utilizing your mind in the manner outlined in earlier chapters, you must start doing what you can where you are and finish what you can where you are. To progress, one must surpass their current location; and an individual cannot surpass their current location if they neglect any tasks related to it. The only people who make progress in the world are those who surpass their current status.

Should a guy fail to fully occupy his current position, it is evident that something is always moving backward. People who don't fully fit in their current roles are a burden on society, the government, business, and industry; others must do the heavy lifting for them at significant financial expenditure. The only people that impede global advancement are those who do not occupy the positions they now occupy; they are from a bygone period, a lesser level of existence, and they have a propensity toward decay. If every individual was smaller than his position, no society could progress; the rule of physical and mental progression governs social evolution. Excess life leads to evolution in the animal kingdom.

An organism develops the organs of a higher plane and gives rise to a new species when it has more life than can be represented in the functions of its own plane. If creatures hadn't more than filled up their spaces, new species would never have arisen. Your ability to become wealthy is contingent upon your application of this concept to your own circumstances. The law is the same for you.

Every day is either a successful day or a day of failure, and the things you seek come from the successful days. If every day is a failure, you can never become wealthy; yet if every day is a success, you cannot fail to get rich. If there is anything you can do today, and you choose not to do it, you have failed in that regard, and the repercussions can be worse than you could have imagined.

Even the smallest action has consequences that you cannot predict, and you are unaware of the mechanisms behind all the forces arranged to operate in your favor. A lot might rely on you carrying out a little deed; it could be the one that unlocks the door to enormous opportunities. You can never know what combinations Supreme Intelligence is creating for you in the realm of things and human events; you may have to wait a long time to acquire what you desire if you ignore or fail to take little action.

Every day, complete all that is possible to accomplish. But there is a caveat or qualifier to the above that you need to be aware of.

You shouldn't overwork yourself or dive headfirst into your company in an attempt to do as many tasks as possible in the quickest amount of time.

You should not attempt to perform a week's worth of work in a single day or attempt to complete today's job tomorrow. The most important thing is not how many things you do, but rather how effective each one is.

Every action is either a success or a failure in and of itself. Every action has inherent effectiveness or inefficiency.

Every ineffective deed is a failure, and if you do ineffective deeds throughout your life, you will fail miserably. If everything you do is ineffective, the more things you do, the worse off you will be.

Conversely, each successful act on your part is a success in and of itself, thus if all of your life's actions are successful, then your whole existence MUST be a success.

Too many things done inefficiently and not enough things done efficiently are the root causes of failure.

You will see that it is a self-evident statement that if you do not commit any inefficient actions, and if you do a sufficient number of efficient acts, you will get affluent. If you can now make every action more efficient, you will once again see that obtaining wealth is really a precise science, much like mathematics.

The crux of the issue therefore becomes whether you can make each individual act stand alone as a success. You can surely do this. Because All Power is collaborating with you and All Power is unbreakable, you can make any act successful. You have the ability to exert power, and all it takes to make an action effective is to apply power to it.

Every action has two possible outcomes: strong or weak. When you behave in a certain way that will lead to wealth, you are behaving with strength. By maintaining your vision and applying all of your faith and purpose to your actions, you can make any act powerful and effective.

It is at this stage when the individuals who divorce mental strength from personal action. They act at one location at one moment, and they employ their mental strength in another location at another time. Because too many of their actions are ineffective, they are not successful in and of themselves. However, if All Power is used to every action, regardless of how routine, then every action will be a success in and of itself. Because success by nature leads to more successes, you will make more and more progress toward your goals and they will make more and more progress toward you.

Keep in mind that effective action has cumulative effects. Since everything has an innate need for more life, when a man starts to pursue a bigger existence, more things gravitate toward him and his desire gains more clout. Every day, do all within your power, and carry out each task as effectively as possible.

When I say that you must keep your vision while doing every act, no matter how tiny or routine, I do not intend to imply that you must always be able to see the vision clearly and in all of its elements. Using your imagination to go out the intricacies of your vision and thinking about them until they are ingrained in your memory should be the task of your free time. Almost all of your free time should be dedicated to this exercise if you want quick results.

By constant contemplation, you will acquire a mental image of what you want—complete with all the fine details—so thoroughly transferred to the mind of Formless Substance that, during working hours, all you have to do is mentally consult the image to inspire faith and purpose and put forth your best effort. Think on the photo throughout your free time until it fills your mind to the point where you can comprehend it with ease. Its dazzling promises will enthrall you to such an extent that the very notion of it will awaken the greatest forces inside you.

Let's go over our curriculum once again and bring it up to the current point by making a few minor adjustments to the concluding remarks.

All things are formed of a thinking substance that, in its primordial form, fills the voids in the cosmos and pervades everything. In this substance a mind generates the object it is seeing. Man has the ability to shape things in his mind and can bring about the creation of those forms by imprinting his thoughts into formless matter. To do this, man must transform his thinking from one of competition to one of creativity; he must visualize his goals and act on them with confidence and purpose, completing each task at hand quickly and effectively.

CHAPTER 13:

Entering The Right Business.

The ability to possess the necessary skills in a fully developed condition is a prerequisite for success in any given industry.

No one can be a successful music teacher without having strong musical ability; no one can be very successful in any mechanical vocation without having strong technical ability; and no one can be successful in mercantile endeavors without having tact and strong commercial ability. However, having the skills necessary for your specific line of work in a fully formed condition does not guarantee financial success. Among the impoverished are musicians with exceptional skill; among the skilled craftsmen, such as carpenters and blacksmiths, who do not become wealthy; and among the merchants who have considerable resources to deal with unsuccessful folks.

The various faculties are tools. It is necessary to have excellent tools, but it is also necessary to utilize the tools correctly. With the right equipment, one guy may construct a beautiful piece of furniture using a sharp saw, square, excellent plane, and so on; another man can use the same tools to try to replicate the piece, but the result will be a mess. He lacks the knowledge necessary to effectively utilize quality tools.

Your mind's many capacities are the tools you need to execute the task that will make you wealthy; if you enter a field for which you have strong mental preparation, success will come more easily. In general, you will perform best in the industry that best utilizes your greatest skills and is a natural match for you. However, this assertion is not without restrictions. No guy should believe that the inclinations he was born with permanently determine his career.

It is possible to become wealthy in ANY industry, even if you lack the requisite skill set.

Developing that skill just requires you to create your own tools rather than relying only on your innate abilities. You will find it easier to thrive in a career where you already possess the necessary abilities in a well-developed condition, but you can excel in any career since you are capable of developing any ability, even if it is just basic.

In terms of effort, you will get wealthy most quickly if you pursue your most suited course of action; yet, you will achieve financial satisfaction if you pursue your passion. Living is about doing what you want to do, and if we are forced to do things we dislike or are never able to do what we want to do, then life is not really satisfying. It is also a given that you possess the ability to do everything you set your mind to; your desire to achieve anything is evidence of this.

Power manifests itself as desire. The skill that seeks expression and growth is the ability to perform music, just as the desire to create mechanical devices is the talent that seeks expression and development in mechanics. When there is a strong want to do anything, it is a sure sign that there is strong power to accomplish that thing; it only needs to be developed and utilized in the right way. In contrast, if there is no strength, either developed or undeveloped, to do that thing, there is never any desire to do that thing.

When all else is equal, it is ideal to choose the company for which you have the most developed skill; nevertheless, if a certain kind of employment is what you really want to do, then that should be your ultimate goal. You have the freedom to pursue your interests, and it is your prerogative to work in a field or pursue a career that you find most agreeable and fulfilling.

You shouldn't have to do anything you dislike, and you shouldn't do it unless it's a way to get you to accomplish what you want to do. You might have to spend some time doing something you dislike if previous mistakes have put you in an unfavorable situation or setting. However, you can enjoy the task by realizing that it is paving the way for you to eventually be able to do what you want to do.

Do not rush into attempting to enter another profession if you believe that your current one is not the appropriate fit for you. Generally speaking, expansion is the greatest approach to improve a company or environment. If an opportunity arises and you believe, after careful thought, that it is the correct chance, don't be afraid to make a sudden and drastic change. However, never act in a sudden or radical way if you are unsure whether it is the proper thing to do. On the creative realm, time never stands still, and opportunities abound.

It will become clear to you that you never need to behave hurriedly once you break free from your competitive mindset. There is plenty for everyone, therefore nobody else will stop you from achieving your goals. There is plenty of time, so if one spot is occupied, a better one will open up for you a little later. Wait if you are unsure. Rely on thinking about your goal, grow in faith and purpose, and, above all, practice thankfulness throughout periods of uncertainty and uncertainty.

You may create such a strong connection with the Supreme when you spend a day or two thinking about what you desire and really thanking God for granting it to you, that when you do act, you won't make any mistakes. There is a mind that is all-knowing, and if you have a great sense of appreciation, you may unite with this mind via faith and the desire to progress in life. Errors stem from rushing things, acting out of uncertainty or fear, or failing to remember the Right Motive—more life for everyone, less for none.

Opportunities will present themselves to you in greater measure as you continue on the Certain Way; thus, you will need to remain steadfast in your faith and purpose and maintain a strong relationship with the All Mind via respectful thankfulness. Every day, perform to the best of your abilities, but do it without hurry, anxiety, or fear. Travel at your own pace, but never rush.

Keep in mind that the instant you start rushing, you stop being a creator and return to being a competitor, returning to the previous level of existence. Anytime you see yourself rushing, stop, focus on the picture in your mind of what you desire, and start expressing gratitude for what you are receiving. Your faith will always

be strengthened and your purpose will always
be renewed when you practice gratitude.

CHAPTER 14:

The Impression Of Increase.

Your current activities must be related to the company you are now involved in, regardless of whether you decide to change careers. By executing your everyday job in a certain way and making good use of the company you are currently established in, you may enter the industry of your choice. If your company involves interacting with other guys, either in person or by correspondence, your primary goal should be to instill a sense of confidence in their thoughts.

All men and all women are searching for increase; it is the need of their Formless Intelligence, which is yearning for more complete manifestation. All of nature is driven by an innate urge for growth; it is the universe's basic motivation. The drive for growth is the foundation of all human endeavors; humans want to have more food, clothing, better housing, luxury, beauty, knowledge, pleasure, and life itself.

Every living thing is subject to this need for constant progress; when life growth stops, disintegration and death occur simultaneously. Because man understands this in his heart, he will always be looking for more. In the parable of the talents, Jesus lays out this rule of eternal increase: only those who gain more get to keep what they have, while those who have nothing will have even their possessions taken away from them. The typical desire for more riches is only an aim for a more affluent existence, not anything bad or disgusting.

Men and women are drawn to those who can provide them with more resources since it is a fundamental aspect of their character. By adhering to the Specific Method outlined in the previous pages, you are continuously improving yourself and providing value to everyone you interact with. You are a creative hub from which everyone receives an increase.

You should be certain of this and assure every man, woman, and kid you encounter of it. Regardless of the size of the transaction—even if it's just you selling a young kid a bar of candy—incorporate growth and make sure the consumer is pleased with the idea.

Make it seem as if you are an advancing man who advances everyone you come into contact with by projecting an air of progress in all you do. Give the idea of growth even to those you meet socially, without any commercial intention, and without attempting to sell them anything.

You may provide this impression by allowing your unwavering belief that you are on the Way of Increase guide, fill, and permeate every action you do. Pursue all your endeavors with the steadfast belief that you are a forward-thinking individual who is propelling progress for everybody. Feel as if you are becoming wealthy and that by doing so, you are benefiting everyone else. Honest faith is never arrogant, so don't gloat about your accomplishments or speak about them too much.

Anywhere you find a boastful individual, there's a scared, uncertain person below. Just have faith, and let it shine through in every interaction; let every gesture, tone, and expression convey the calm confidence that you are growing rich, or that you are already wealthy. Others will sense an increase in your presence and become drawn to you once again, thus words won't be needed to express this sensation to them. You have to make such an impression on them that they believe joining you would benefit them personally. Make sure the use value you provide them outweighs the money you are collecting from them.

Be really proud of what you're doing and tell everyone about it, and you'll never run out of clients. Where there is growth, people will go; and the Supreme, who knows everything and wants increase in everything, will draw those who have never heard of you. Your company will grow quickly, and you'll be shocked by the unanticipated advantages that will follow. Every day, you will have the opportunity to form more advantageous combinations, get more benefits, and, if you so choose, advance into a more amiable profession.

While pursuing all of this, you must never lose sight of your goals or your belief that you will succeed in achieving them. Permit me to provide one more warning about motivations.

Avoid giving in to the sneaky desire to rule other guys. Nothing is more enjoyable to an undeveloped or partly formed intellect than to exert dominance or authority over others. The scourge of the world has been the ambition to govern for one's own selfish satisfaction. For innumerable centuries, kings and lords have shed blood on the planet during their conflicts to expand their domains—not in an effort to increase the life expectancy of everyone, but rather in an attempt to increase their own authority.

The primary driving force behind today's corporate and industrial worlds is still the same: men gather armies of money and destroy millions of lives and hearts in a crazed attempt to gain control over others. Like political rulers, commercial kings are motivated by a desire for power.

Jesus saw the driving force of that wicked society He aimed to destroy in this yearning for dominance. Read Matthew 23 and observe how He depicts the Pharisees' desire to be called "Masters," to occupy positions of authority, to rule over others, and to place burdens on the backs of the less fortunate. Also, take note of how He contrasts this desire for dominance with the fraternal pursuit of the Common Good that He calls His disciples to.

Watch out for the need to assume power, to establish oneself as a "master," to stand out from the crowd, to dazzle people with ostentatious displays, and so on.

The competitive mind is different from the creative mind in that it aspires to dominate others. It is not at all necessary to rule over other people in order to control your environment and destiny. In fact, when you get caught up in the race for the top, fate and environment start to control you, and becoming wealthy becomes a matter of luck and conjecture.

Watch out for a competitive mindset! The favorite quote of the late "Golden Rule" Jones of Toledo, "What I want for myself, I want for everybody," is the best way to express the idea of creative action.

CHAPTER 15:

The Advancing Man.

The previous chapter's advice holds true for both professional and wage-earning men as well as those involved in mercantile enterprise.

Regardless of your profession—medicine, education, or religion—if you can prolong someone's life and help them realize it, people will be drawn to you and you will become wealthy. Patients will flock to the physician who has a vision of himself as a great and successful healer and who works toward the full realization of that vision with faith and purpose, as explained in previous chapters. This physician will have such a close relationship with the Source of Life that he will be extraordinarily successful.

The medical practitioner has the greatest potential to implement the principles presented in this book. It makes no difference whose school of thought the practitioner comes from; the idea of healing is universal and accessible to everyone. No matter what cures he may use, the Advancing Man in medicine, who maintains a clear mental picture of himself as successful and who abides by the rules of faith, purpose, and thankfulness, will heal every curable case he takes on.

The world is crying out for a priest who can impart the actual science of abundant life to his listeners in the religious sector. A congregation will always be available to someone who understands the intricacies of the science of wealth accumulation, as well as the related sciences of greatness, health, and earning love, and who imparts these subtleties from the pulpit. The world needs this gospel; it will multiply life, people will happily hear it, and they will generously support the one who shares it.

Now what's required is a pulpit presentation of the science of life. We are looking for preachers who can not only explain things to us, but who can also demonstrate them for us. To teach us how to achieve these things, we need the preacher who will also be wealthy, well-groomed, famous, and adored. When he arrives, he will have a sizable and devoted following.

The same is true of the educator, who has the ability to instill in the kids a sense of faith and a desire to improve life. He is never going to be "out of a job." And any educator who shares this conviction and purpose may impart it to his students; if it is a part of his own practice and life, he cannot resist imparting it to them. All lawyers, dentists, real estate agents, and insurance agents share the same truths as teachers, preachers, and doctors.

I have outlined a failsafe, non-failing course of integrated mental and personal activity. Anyone who follows these guidelines diligently, consistently, and exactly will become wealthy. Getting wealthy is a precise science; the law of the Increase of Life operates with the same mathematical certainty as the rule of gravity.

This will apply to the wage earner's situation just as it does to any of the others stated. Don't let the fact that you work in an environment with few prospects for growth, low pay, and expensive living expenses make you believe that you have no possibility of becoming wealthy. Create a clear mental picture of what you desire, then start acting with confidence and intention.

Work as hard as you can, every day, and do each task in a way that is ideally successful; infuse your success and desire for wealth into everything that you do. However, avoid doing this only to gain favor with your employer or those in positions of authority in the hopes that they would recognize your hard work and promote you—it is unlikely that they will.

It is not in the employer's best interest to promote a guy who is content to be a "good" worker who does his job to the best of his abilities since he is more useful where he is. More is required for progress to be secured than just being overweight.

The guy who is too large for his position and knows exactly what he wants to be—who is willing to BE that person and who knows he can become that person—is the one who is sure to succeed.

Instead of filling the position with the intention of appeasing your boss, aim to go up the ladder for yourself. Maintain the belief and intention to grow before, during, and after work hours. Make sure that everyone who comes into touch with you—whether they are a foreman, a fellow worker, or a social acquaintance—feels the strength of purpose emanating from you. This will give everyone a feeling of development and growth. You will attract guys, and you will quickly notice a chance to pursue a different career if there is no room for growth in your current one.

There is a Power which never fails to offer opportunity to the Advancing Man who is advancing in compliance to rule. If you behave in a certain way, God cannot help but assist you; He must help Himself in order to help you.

Nothing about your condition or the state of the industry can hold you back. If working for the steel trust isn't your thing, you can make a lot of money on a ten-acre farm. If you start moving in the right direction, you'll be able to leave the "clutches" of the steel trust and go to the farm or another location of your choosing.

The steel trust would quickly find itself in a difficult situation if a few thousand of its workers followed the Certain Way; it would either have to provide its working men additional opportunities or go out of business. No one is required to work for a trust; trusts can only maintain men in supposedly hopeless situations for as long as there are men who are either too lazy or too uneducated to understand the science of becoming wealthy.

Once you start thinking and behaving in this manner, your faith and sense of purpose will help you see opportunities to improve your situation quickly. These prospects will materialize quickly because the Supreme, who is at work in all things and on your behalf, will bring them to you. When the chance to become someone you've always wanted to be presents itself, seize it without delay. You should never wait to be all that you can be. It will serve as a springboard to other opportunities.

For a guy living a progressive life, there can never be a shortage of options in this cosmos. The universe is designed so that everything will work out for his benefit and be for his benefit; if he behaves and thinks in a particular way, he will undoubtedly become wealthy. Therefore, wage-earning men and women should carefully read this book and confidently follow its recommended course of action because it will work.

CHAPTER 16:

Some Cautions, And Concluding Observations.

The concept that there is a precise science to being wealthy will be laughed at by many. They will argue that social and political structures need to alter before a significant portion of the population can become competent, believing that there is a finite quantity of money. However, this is untrue.

It is true that the majority are kept in poverty by the current administrations, but this is because the masses do not behave and think in a certain way. Governments and industrial systems cannot stop the people from moving ahead as this book suggests; instead, all systems must be adjusted to allow for this forward motion. Nothing could possible hold individuals in poverty if they have an advancing mind, faith that they can become wealthy, and a clear goal to achieve that goal.

People may follow the Certain manner at any time and under any kind of government to become wealthy; and when a significant enough number of people follow this path under any kind of government, they will alter the system in a manner that makes room for more people.

It is better for others when more men get wealthy on the creative plane than it is for others when more men become wealthy on the competitive level. The only way to save the economy for the majority of people is to encourage a lot of people to follow the scientific process outlined in this book and become wealthy. These will lead the way and motivate others by inspiring a desire for genuine life, the belief that it is possible, and the drive to achieve it.

For now, however, it's sufficient to know that neither capitalism nor the competitive nature of the industrial system can prevent you from becoming wealthy. You'll transcend all of them and join a different realm once you step into the creative plane of mind.

However, keep in mind that you must always think creatively; you will never, ever be duped into thinking of the supply as being limited or into responding in a way that is morally competitive. If you find yourself slipping back into old thinking patterns, catch yourself right away because the Mind of the Whole will not cooperate with you while you are in a competitive frame of mind.

Save your time and effort on making plans for future emergency response, unless there are urgent policies that need to be followed now. You are focused on completing today's tasks successfully; you don't need to worry about any crises that may happen tomorrow; you can handle them when they arise. If you cannot clearly see that you need to change your route today in order to prevent impending hurdles in your company, then don't worry about how you will overcome them.

Regardless of how massive an obstacle may seem from a distance, you will discover that if you continue in the Certain Way, it will either vanish as you get closer to it or that a path will emerge to go over, through, or around it. A person pursuing wealth by completely scientific means cannot be defeated by any set of circumstances. No law-abiding man or woman can fail to become wealthy, any more than a person can multiply two by two and not obtain four.

Ignore fears of impending catastrophes, roadblocks, panic attacks, or unfavorable events; you have plenty of time to deal with these things when they arise in the here and now, and you'll discover that every challenge comes with the resources to overcome it. Be careful with words. Never talk in a dejected or depressing manner about yourself, your circumstances, or anything else.

Never acknowledge the chance of failing or imply that failure is a possibility in speech. Never describe the current state of affairs as difficult or the state of business as uncertain. For those in a competitive industry, times could be challenging and uncertain, but this need never apply to you because you have the ability to create whatever you choose and are fearless. It is when others are struggling and doing poorly in business that you will discover the most opportunity.

Teach yourself to perceive the world as something that is becoming and becoming, and to understand that seeming evil is just the state of being underdeveloped. Talk only about progress; anything less is a denial of your faith, and losing faith is the result of doing so. Never give in to feelings of disappointment. It's possible that you'll anticipate something at a certain moment and it won't arrive when you want it to, which will make you feel unsuccessful.

But if you stick to your beliefs, you'll discover that the failure is simply visible. Continue in a certain direction, and even if you don't get what you're hoping for, you'll get something so much better that you'll realize the seeming setback turned out to be a huge triumph.

A scientific student was determined to create a certain business combination that he thought would be very desired, and he spent many weeks working towards it. The item failed in an entirely unexplainable manner at the critical moment; it was as if some invisible force had been acting covertly against him. Rather of becoming disheartened, he expressed gratitude to God for overriding his desire and continued with a thankful mindset. A few weeks later, he was presented with an opportunity so much better than the first one, and he realized that he had been saved from losing the bigger good by not becoming involved in the smaller one by a Mind that understood more than he did.

If you maintain your faith, stay true to your mission, practice appreciation, and do everything that you can each day—each distinct act successfully—that is how every seeming setback will turn out for you. Failure stems from not asking for enough; if you persevere, you will undoubtedly get more than you were hoping for. Remember this.

You are not going to fail because you are not talented enough to do what you want to achieve. If you continue as I have instructed, you will acquire every skill required to carry out your duties. The science of developing talent is beyond the purview of this book, yet it is just as definite and straightforward as the path to financial success.

But don't pause or falter for fear that you won't be able to succeed when you get to a specific point; just keep moving forward, and you'll be given the ability when you get there. You have access to the same pool of talent that allowed the ignorant Lincoln to carry out the greatest piece of single-handed government work ever seen; you may utilize all of human knowledge to apply wisdom to the tasks entrusted to you. Continue with complete trust.

Examine this book. Until you have grasped all of its concepts, make it your constant friend. You would do well to give up most leisure activities and pleasures while you are becoming firmly entrenched in your religion. You should also avoid locations where lectures or sermons promoting beliefs at odds with these are given. Avoid reading contradictory or negative material and avoid engaging in debates about it. Read virtually nothing else outside the authors listed in the Preface. Make the most of your free time by reading this book, reflecting on your vision, and practicing appreciation. It includes all the information you want to understand the science of being wealthy, and the next chapter provides a summary of all the key points.

CHAPTER 17:

A Synopsis Of The Science Of Getting Rich.

All things are formed of a thinking substance that, in its primordial form, fills the voids in the cosmos and pervades everything. In this substance, a mind generates the object it is seeing. Man is able to shape things in his mind, and he can create things by imprinting his thoughts into formless substances. Man cannot be in harmony with the Formless Intelligence, which is always creative and never competing in spirit, until he transcends from the competitive to the creative mind.

By expressing heartfelt thanks for everything that the Formless Substance has given him, man might achieve complete harmony with it. Gratitude makes the intellect of man one with the intelligence of Substance, allowing the Formless to hear what man has to say. The only way for man to stay on the creative level is to merge with the Formless Intelligence via a persistent, profound sense of appreciation.

Man must create a distinct mental picture of what he wants to be, do, or become. He must then hold this mental picture in his mind and express his sincere gratitude to the Supreme for fulfilling all of his wishes. If a guy wants to become wealthy, he should use his free time to reflect on his vision and to express sincere appreciation for the gift of reality. It is impossible to overstate the significance of regularly reflecting on the mental picture in conjunction with unshakable trust and heartfelt thankfulness. This is how the creative forces are activated and the Formless is given the impression.

The established pathways of economic and social order, as well as natural development, are used by the creative force. The individual who follows the preceding directions and whose trust does not waver will undoubtedly get all that is contained in his mental vision. He will get what he wants by using the channels of established trade and business.

Man must be active in order to get his own when it comes to him, and this activity can only include more than occupying his current position. He has to remain focused on his goal of becoming wealthy by the manifestation of his inner vision. And he has to do all that is possible each day, making sure that each task is completed well. In order for each transaction to result in more life, he must provide each guy a use value that exceeds the financial value he gets. Additionally, he must maintain the Advancing Thought that the impression of Increase will be shared with everyone he encounters.

Those who follow the above guidelines will undoubtedly become wealthy, and their wealth will be precisely proportionate to how clear-cut their vision is, how unwavering their purpose is, how steadfast their faith is, and how grateful they are.

CONCLUSION

Ultimately, an examination of "The Psychology of Becoming a Millionaire: The Science of Breaking Free From Paycheck-to-Paycheck Cycle and Joining the Ranks of the Rich Elite" demonstrates how mentality, routines, and calculated financial preparation interact in a variety of intricate ways. The path to financial prosperity is heavily impacted by one's psychological perspective on money and success rather than being primarily determined by outside variables like income or good fortune.

Millionaires who are able to escape the pattern of living paycheck to paycheck often have similar psychological characteristics. They have a proactive mentality, seeing barriers as chances rather than roadblocks. Their capacity to have a healthy relationship with money and see it as a tool for financial freedom rather than merely a means of subsistence is essential. Furthermore, they can successfully manage the ever-changing world of personal finance and investing because to their dedication to lifelong learning and adaptation.

It's also critical to get beyond the psychological obstacles connected to financial success. In order to become a billionaire, a person has to challenge their limiting beliefs, build resilience, and have a healthy appetite for risk. A mentality change from scarcity to plenty is necessary to escape the paycheck-to-paycheck cycle. This involves seeing and actively pursuing chances for wealth development.

Planning strategically with regard to finances is also essential to this life-changing experience. Millionaires use complex investing methods, diversify their portfolios, and recognize the power of compounding in addition to budgeting and saving. The science of wealth accumulation entails making well-informed decisions, defining exacting goals, and carrying out financial plans with discipline.

However, there are obstacles in the way of becoming a billionaire. As people deal with unpredicted losses, market volatility, and economic uncertainty, endurance and patience become vital qualities. Resilience psychology combined with a calculated attitude to conquering challenges sets apart people who escape poverty and get to the top of the affluent class.

"The Psychology of Becoming a Millionaire" essentially highlights how thinking, habits, and financial methods interact in a complex way while pursuing financial success. It acts as a guide for those who want to break free from the pattern of living paycheck to paycheck and become wealthy elite members. Through comprehending and using the psychological components included in accumulating money, people may set out on a transforming path towards achieving financial independence and becoming members of the elite billionaire club.